Castles of
Wales

Rhodri Owen

GRAFFEG

Contents

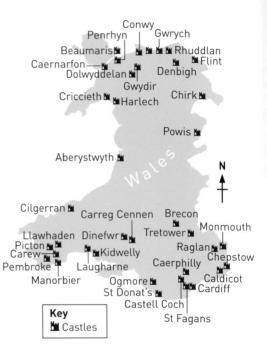

Conwy
Penrhyn   Gwrych
Beaumaris   Rhuddlan
Caernarfon   Flint
Dolwyddelan   Denbigh
Gwydir   Chirk
Criccieth   Harlech
Powis
Aberystwyth   Wales
N
Cilgerran   Carreg Cennen   Brecon
Llawhaden   Dinefwr   Tretower   Monmouth
Picton   Raglan
Carew   Kidwelly   Chepstow
Pembroke   Laugharne   Caerphilly
Manorbier   Caldicot
Ogmore   Cardiff
St Donat's   Castell Coch
St Fagans

Key
Castles

Introduction

The story of the castles of Wales is the story of those who built them, lived in them and fought over them. For four centuries after the turn of the first millennium this rugged and mountainous land became a battleground as the Welsh fought to defend their native home against invading Norman lords and English monarchs.

The struggle for control over strategic locations from Chepstow to Beaumaris sparked an unparalleled era of castle building. A dream of independence led the Welsh princes Llywelyn ap Iorwerth and Llywelyn ap Gruffudd to construct and defend their own magnificent fortresses, like those at Dolwyddelan, Criccieth or Carreg Cennen. But the dream ended with Welsh rebel forces having to rise up against strongholds such as those at Caernarfon, Harlech or Caerphilly that were built in greater size and number to subdue them.

After the fall of the last Welsh prince, Owain Glyndŵr, the castles of Wales were caught up in two centuries of English domestic warfare. The Wars of the Roses and the wanton destruction wrought after the English Civil War extracted a heavy toll.

Some 600 castles were built across Wales, of which more than 400 remain, but this amounts to an extraordinary architectural legacy that, in north Wales alone, has received global recognition from UNESCO, the United Nations Educational, Scientific and Cultural Organisation.

Whether left to decay into romantic ruins or else converted into stately mansions and inhabited to this day, each castle has an enduring and engrossing story to tell. There are tales of conspiracy, treason, kidnap and murder; legends of a giant king, a Shakespearean tragic hero and a real-life warrior princess; histories of high art, elegant gardens and opulent architecture.

In pictures and words, *Castles of Wales* offers a glimpse into the drama of thirty-seven of these towering monuments.

North Wales
Beaumaris Castle

Castle Street, Beaumaris, Gwynedd, LL58 8AP.
Constructed 1295-1330.
UNESCO World Heritage Site.
www.cadw.wales.gov.uk.

....

Built close to sea level on the 'fair marsh' from which it derives its name, Beaumaris Castle looks back from Anglesey's eastern shore across the Menai Strait to the peaks of Snowdonia.

Beaumaris was the last of King Edward I's 'Iron Ring' castles to be built. Like Conwy, Harlech and Caernarfon, with which it shares UNESCO World Heritage Site status, it was designed by his master mason, James of St George.

Construction began in 1295, thirteen years after Llywelyn ap Gruffudd's death confirmed Edward I's conquest of Wales and the same year that the uprising of Madog ap Llywelyn, self-proclaimed Prince of Wales, was quashed. With the attention of the king and his chief castle builder having moved on to Scotland, work here continued intermittently until the money ran out in 1330 and was never completed.

Geometrically symmetrical, with six towers and two D-shaped gatehouse keeps, Beaumaris had four concentric rings while a tidal dock allowed for direct supply by sea, but despite its formidable defences and area span the castle never reached the intimidating height of its mainland counterparts.

The castle's garrison repelled an attack by a Scottish raiding party in 1381, but in 1403 it was besieged and taken by rebels loyal to Owain Glyndŵr, who held it for two years.

Although Beaumaris Castle had fallen into decay by the turn of the seventeenth century, it was restored and garrisoned by Thomas Bulkeley for the Royalist cause in the English Civil War. The castle was surrendered to the Parliamentarians in 1646 but escaped the slighting customarily handed out by Oliver Cromwell to other castles in Wales.

In the autumn of 1832, at the age of thirteen, the future Queen Victoria attended an eisteddfod at Beaumaris Castle during a prolonged stay in north Wales.

•••

Pages 4-5: The main entrance at Beaumaris.
Pages 6-7: Beaumaris Castle walls.

Caernarfon Castle

Castle Ditch, Caernarfon, Gwynedd,
LL55 2AY.
Constructed 1283-1330.
UNESCO World Heritage Site.
www.cadw.wales.gov.uk.

**Modelled on the Roman walls of
Constantinople, now Istanbul in Turkey,
Caernarfon Castle is arguably the most
striking of all King Edward I's castles and
certainly one of the best preserved.**

The long seven-towered castle rises up
from the harbourside at the mouth of the

River Seiont and looks across the Menai Strait to the Isle of Anglesey, or Ynys Môn, off the north-western tip of Wales.

Caernarfon takes its name from the Roman fort Segontium. Built nearby in 77 AD, this important military base and administrative centre was referred to in the Welsh expression *'y gaer yn Arfon'* as 'the fortress alongside Môn'.

A motte and bailey fort stood next to the Seiont in the late eleventh century, raised by the Norman lord Hugh D'Avranches, a close ally of William the Conqueror, after he took control of Gwynedd.

By 1115 the princes of Wales had wrestled it back, and both Llywelyn ap Iorwerth and his grandson, Llywelyn ap Gruffudd, used the fort as a residence. But the death of Llywelyn Ein Llyw Olaf (Llywelyn the Last) in 1282 marked the completion of Edward I's efforts to bring Wales under his authority and construction began on an 'Iron Ring' of castles around his prize.

As a prince in 1271-2, 'Longshanks', as he was known due to his height, had journeyed across Europe to crusade in the Holy Land. One can imagine how the grandeur of the city walls constructed by the Roman emperor Constantine the Great

might have stayed in his mind and proved influential when it came to building his own fortifications.

On his return from the Middle East, Edward visited Savoy, now in south-eastern France, and may have been equally impressed with the work of an architect from that region.

James of St George, or Jacques de Saint-Georges D'Ésperanche, was later appointed Master of the King's Works in Wales and was responsible for many of Edward I's castles, including those also recognised by UNESCO at Beaumaris, Harlech and Conwy. He began work on Caernarfon Castle in 1283.

The castle contained two main courtyards and was built in a figure of eight shape, with long curtain walls, twin-towered gates and polygonal rather than circular towers. By paying homage in its design to the Romans who had conquered Wales before him, Edward I was clearly intending to make a bold statement of his own. At Caernarfon he would build a castle to serve as a military and administrative powerhouse. The birth of his son, later King Edward II, here in 1284 reinforced the king's vision of a royal palace from where a new sort of prince would rule over Wales.

under attack from Welsh rebels, those led by Owain Glyndŵr in the early years of the fifteenth century, it was strong enough to stand firm.

By the Tudor era Caernarfon's importance had dwindled and its castle had begun to deteriorate. At the onset of the English Civil War it was quickly licked back into shape and garrisoned for the king before it was besieged three times, surrendering in 1646.

In 1911, more than 600 years after the young Prince Edward was offered up as a first non-native Prince of Wales, Caernarfon Castle hosted a ceremony granting the same title to another Prince Edward, later King Edward VIII. The ceremony was repeated in 1969 with the investiture of Prince Charles, later King Charles III.

The Welsh had other ideas, however, and in 1294 an army raised by Madog ap Llywelyn breached the castle's unfinished defences, holding out until Edward I replied with a greater show of force. Construction work resumed and continued until 1330. When the castle next came

....

Pages 8-9: The castle seen from across Caernarfon Bay.
Pages 10-11: The interior courtyard.
Pages 12-13: A view of one of the castle's distinctive towers overlooking the River Seiont.

Conwy Castle

Rose Hill Street, Conwy, LL32 8AY.
Constructed 1283-1287.
UNESCO World Heritage Site.
www.cadw.wales.gov.uk.

....

The energy with which King Edward I created his 'Iron Ring' of castles around north Wales is evident at Conwy Castle, which took just four years to build. Towering above the west bank of the River Conwy, the castle was the work of Edward I's architect and master mason, James of St George. It was placed, contemptuously, on the site of an abbey founded by Llywelyn ap Iorwerth and a residence belonging to Llywelyn ap Gruffudd.

Construction began in 1283 and ended in 1287, by which time the castle's eight towers, two wards and a town wall more than one kilometre long had been completed.

Within the fortress James created a suite of royal apartments which survive in remarkable condition, but which Edward I only visited once, while putting down Madog ap Llywelyn's uprising of 1294-5.

In 1399 King Richard II stayed at Conwy Castle shortly before being arrested and deposed by Henry Bolingbroke. Later, in 1401, the castle fell to supporters of Owain Glyndŵr, who tricked their way inside dressed as workmen and carrying concealed weapons.

The castle was garrisoned by Royalists during the English Civil War but was besieged and fell to the Parliamentarians in 1646.

With its own towers echoing those of the castle, Thomas Telford's suspension bridge was added in 1826, taking as long to build as the castle itself had 500 years earlier. Together with Beaumaris, Caernarfon and Harlech, Conwy Castle is a UNESCO World Heritage Site.

....

Pages 14-15: Designed by Thomas Telford and constructed from 1822-1826, the suspension bridge gives pedestrian access to Conwy Castle.

Pages 16-17: Conwy Castle from across the harbour.

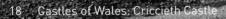

Criccieth Castle

Castle Street, Criccieth, Gwynedd, LL52 0DP.
Constructed 13th century.
www.cadw.wales.gov.uk.

....

Commanding a panoramic view across Tremadog Bay from a high, rocky headland on the southern coast of the Llŷn Peninsula, Criccieth Castle was built in around the 1220s by Llywelyn ap Iorwerth, prince of Gwynedd and later most of Wales.

Intended as a robust royal residence, it boasted characteristically Welsh D-shaped gatehouse towers and was just one of several castles raised to defend Llywelyn's borders.

In 1239 Criccieth Castle served as a prison to Llywelyn's son, Gruffudd, after he fell out with his half-brother Dafydd, Llywelyn's chosen heir. Twenty years later, Maredudd ap Rhys Gryg, a prince of Deheubarth tried for treason in 1259 after switching allegiance to King Henry III, was also imprisoned here.

In the 1260s an outer ward was added to the castle by Llywelyn's grandson, Llywelyn ap Gruffudd, who under the Treaty of Montgomery seven years later was officially recognised as Prince of Wales by King Henry III.

When King Edward I began his conquest of Wales in 1277, Criccieth remained safe deep within Welsh-held territory. But after Llywelyn's death in 1282, Edward I's army pushed into Gwynedd and the castle fell, with repairs being undertaken to help strengthen his grip on the territory. Criccieth was further fortified by the English during Edward I's castle building spree at the end of the thirteenth century. In 1284, following Edward I's last visit to Criccieth, he declared it a Free Borough. Attacked by Welsh forces during Madog ap Llywelyn's uprising of 1294-5, its waterfront location proved crucial, as the ability to resupply by sea meant the garrison was able to withstand a lengthy siege.

In 1359 'Syr Hywel y Fwyall', nicknamed 'Hywel of the Battleaxe' for his bravery on the battlefields of France, was appointed constable of Criccieth Castle, a position rarely conferred upon a Welshman at that time and one he held until his death in 1381.

Criccieth Castle's next taste of action came after Owain Glyndŵr, a descendant of the princes of Powys, raised his standard at Glyndyfrdwy in Denbighshire on 16 September 1400, signalling the start of a fifteen-year war against King Henry IV.

Castle after castle across north-west Wales fell to his men, with just the English garrisons at Aberystwyth, Harlech and Criccieth holding out until 1404 when, with Glyndŵr by now the de facto ruler of Wales, the last native prince, all three succumbed.

Criccieth, held by Roger Acton with fifty archers, fell in the spring after a blockade at sea by a French fleet in support of Glyndŵr. Unable to resupply, Acton surrendered. Glyndŵr's men demolished much of the castle, set the rest of it on fire and then burned the surrounding town.

Criccieth Castle was never rebuilt, minor repairs only coming in the 19th century, and so after just 175 years a castle built by one great Welsh prince had been destroyed by another.

The castle was in the hands of the crown until 1858, when it was sold to William Orsby-Gore MP, second Baron Harlech, eventually being turned over to the state for conservation and maintainance in 1933. Cadw, the Welsh agency for historic monuments, now preserves the site, with a visitor centre welcoming the public to explore and take in its significant views.

··

Pages 18-19: Criccieth Castle occupies a rocky peninsula overlooking Tremadog Bay. Page 20: The D-shaped towers of the gatehouse.

Denbigh Castle

Castle Hill, Denbigh, Denbighshire,
LL16 3NB.
Constructed 1282-1311.
www.cadw.wales.gov.uk.

....

As the town of Denbigh in Clwyd gets its name from the Welsh term *dinbych*, or 'little fortress', it is clear that a number of strongholds may have existed on Caledfryn Hill long before the sizeable castle whose ruins are visible today.

One of these fortresses served as the *llys* or court of Dafydd ap Gruffudd, grandson of Llywelyn ap Iorwerth. Dafydd's uprising against the English in 1282 was swiftly put down and led to the death of his brother Llywelyn, Prince of Wales, the same year. Dafydd's fortress was captured and granted to Henry de Lacy, a close ally of King Edward I, who began building a castle in its place with the help of Edward I's chief architect, James of St George.

Construction was delayed in 1294 when the half-built castle was briefly captured by Madog ap Llywelyn's rebel force before being won back. Following this, Henry de Lacy's appetite for the project was sapped by the accidental death of his son, Edmund, who drowned in the castle well, and the building was still unfinished when de Lacy himself died in 1311. The castle passed by marriage to Thomas, Earl of Lancaster, but he was beheaded for treason by King Edward II in 1322 and Denbigh Castle was awarded to Hugh Despenser the Younger.

Despenser's custodianship was briefer still. His growing influence over Edward II, whose statue is still visible above the gatehouse, led to his own execution in 1326 and the king's abdication a year later.

In 1400 Denbigh Castle was besieged by Owain Glyndŵr but held out under the command of Sir Henry Percy, known as 'Hotspur' after his battles against the Scots. Percy later transferred his allegiance to Glyndŵr and was killed at the Battle of Shrewsbury in 1403.

Denbigh came under frequent attack by Lancastrian forces during the Wars of the Roses and the castle was in a state of near ruin when the English Civil War began in 1642.

The wealthy Royalist Colonel William Salesbury paid for its defences to be shored up and under his command it survived a lengthy siege by Parliamentarian forces, until in October 1646 King Charles I ordered its surrender.

Denbigh Castle was then used as a prison for Royalist soldiers and was briefly captured during a Royalist uprising in 1659. A year later it was slighted and left to ruin, with much of its masonry used for building work in the town. The castle ruins hosted an eisteddfod in 1828 in the presence of the Duke of Sussex, brother of both King George IV and King William IV.

In the mid-19th century a 'Castle Committee' was created by the town, tasked with maintaining the ruins. The committee leased control of the site and loaned £300 from the Crown to fund repairs in 1879. During the 21st century Denbigh Castle has been maintained by Cadw, the Welsh heritage agency, who invested £600,000 into the castle and walls during the mid-2010s.

••

Page 23: An aerial view of Denbigh Castle.
Pages 24-25: The ruined castle walls.

Dolwyddelan Castle

Off the A470, Dolwyddelan, Conwy,
LL25 0JD.
Constructed c. 1210-1240.
www.cadw.wales.gov.uk.

··

A stirring sight amid the peaks of Snowdonia, rising above the valley of the River Ledr on a rocky outcrop below Moel Siabod, Dolwyddelan Castle was one of a chain of Welsh-built castles guarding a strategically important route through the mountains of north Wales.

Construction began in the early thirteenth century under Llywelyn ap Iorwerth, ruler of Gwynedd, who was born just a mile away at Tomen Castell in around 1173.

From the sheer drama of its location it is clear that Llywelyn Fawr (Llywelyn the Great) intended Dolwyddelan Castle to be nothing less than a visible symbol of raw Welsh power. In contrast to the larger and more uniform Norman or English castles that were built to subdue the Welsh, Dolwyddelan Castle had all the characteristics of a Welsh-built fortress.

It was compact and took maximum advantage of the more impenetrable features of its immediate natural surroundings, such as rocky escarpments and sheer cliffs. Its tower was also rectangular as opposed to circular.

Llywelyn's power base was in Gwynedd, but in time his influence began to spread across Wales. Towards the end of his life his power began to wane and, after his death in 1240, King Henry III took advantage of the moment to seize land in north-eastern Wales.

By the 1260s Llywelyn's grandson, Llywelyn ap Gruffudd, had risen to prominence in both Welsh and English eyes. Officially recognised by Henry III as the Prince of Wales under the Treaty of Montgomery in 1267, Llywelyn continued his grandfather's programme of castle building and refortified Dolwyddelan.

When Henry III died in 1272, Llywelyn refused to pay homage to his son, King Edward I, and in return Edward invaded Wales. Dolwyddelan Castle played no part in the skirmishes of 1277 in which Edward I succeeded in pushing Llywelyn back into the north-west corner of Wales and seized control of the rest. But when Llywelyn was killed fighting the English near Builth Wells in 1282, it was Edward I's turn to take full advantage by pushing into Gwynedd to complete his conquest of Wales.

Dolwyddelan Castle was taken in 1283, and in English hands it was repaired and strengthened. A second rectangular tower was added as the garrison was boosted. In winter the English soldiers wore white so as to be camouflaged amid the snow. Dolwyddelan Castle remained under Edward I's control until 1290, when it was abandoned.

In 1489 the castle was acquired and restored by the Welsh nobleman Maredudd ab Ifan ab Robert, founder of the Wynn family of Gwydir Castle, who added a third storey to the original tower.

In 1848, Dolwyddelan, now a ruin, was bought by Baron Willoughby de Eresby, under whose directions the keep was heavily rebuilt over the course of the next two years, with the addition of floors, walls and battlements in a fanciful rather than historically accurate style. In 1930 Dolwyddelan Castle was put under government protection and has since been looked after by Cadw.

Pages 26-27: The remote Dolwyddelan Castle maintains a prominent place in the landscape.

Page 29: Only one of the castle's rectangular towers remains intact today, with the tower added by King Edward I in the late 12th century having fallen into ruin.

Flint Castle

Castle Road, Flint, Flintshire, CH6 5PE.
Constructed 1277-1284.
www.cadw.wales.gov.uk.

....

Flint Castle, on the shoreline of the Dee Estuary in north-east Wales, has played a fateful part in the history of both the native princes of Wales and the kings of England.

Flint was the first fortress built in King Edward I's plan to wrap an 'Iron Ring' of castles around north Wales. Building began in 1277 as Edward I sought to push along the coastline into the Welsh stronghold of Gwynedd.

In 1282, two years before construction was completed, the castle was attacked during a Welsh revolt led by Dafydd ap Gruffudd. The attack was repelled but it caused his brother Llywelyn ap Gruffudd, Prince of Wales, to join the uprising in which he was killed later the same year.

In 1399 Flint Castle provided the backdrop for an historic meeting between King Richard II and his usurper Henry Bolingbroke. As later dramatised in Act Three, Scene Three of Shakespeare's play

Richard II, Richard is captured near Conwy and brought down from Flint's great Donjon Tower to the outer ward, where he agrees to submit to Bolingbroke. After following him back to London, Richard was imprisoned in the Tower of London and Bolingbroke seized the throne as King Henry IV.

Garrisoned by Royalists in the English Civil War, Flint Castle changed hands several times before it was finally besieged and captured by Parliamentarians in 1646, then slighted.

The castle's outer ward served as a prison in the seventeenth and eighteenth centuries, and in 1910 the site was bought to act as the headquarters for the Fifth (Flintshire) Battalion Royal Welsh Fusiliers during World War One.

....

Pages 30-31: The remains of Flint Castle's east side.

Gwrych Castle

Tan-Y-Gopa Road, Abergele, Conwy,
LL22 8ET.
Constructed 1819-1825.
www.gwrychcastle.co.uk.

**Gwrych Castle, which stands on a wooded
hill overlooking the north Wales coastline
near Abergele, dates back to the early
nineteenth century. It was built on the
site of a derelict Elizabethan country
house, home to the Lloyd family from the
late fifteenth century, by Lloyd Hesketh
Bamford-Hesketh, an industrialist and
antiquary who inherited the estate from
his mother, Frances Lloyd.**

Bamford-Hesketh designed the
castle in the Gothic Revival style with
help from English architects Charles
Augustus Busby and Thomas Rickman.
The foundation stone was laid in 1819 and
the building, which in its pomp boasted
a 460-metre frontage and contained 128
rooms, was completed by 1825. Formal
gardens were added in the 1830s and a
new wing built in the 1840s.

In 1894 the castle passed down to Bamford-Hesketh's heir, his granddaughter Winifred, the Countess of Dundonald. A Welsh-speaking patron of the arts who was installed as a bard at the 1910 National Eisteddfod, the countess ran the family estate herself and set up two military hospitals during World War One.

After housing 200 Jewish child war refugees as part of Operation Kindertransport during World War Two, Gwrych was sold by the Dundonalds in 1946. It was opened to the public but gradually fell into decline by the 1980s.

On the point of ruin, it was acquired in 2018 by the Gwrych Castle Preservation Trust, a charity set up by archaeological historian Dr Mark Baker to oversee its restoration.

Pages 32-33: The approach to Gwrych Castle, which sits on a 286-acre estate. Pages 34-35: Though constructed in the 19th century, Gwyrch Castle was one of the first attempts at replicating medieval architecture in Europe.

Gwydir Castle

Llanrwst, Conwy, LL26 0PN.
Constructed c. 1500, with later additions.
www.gwydircastle.co.uk.

···

Gwydir Castle could be more accurately described as a Tudor house than a castle, but due to its strategic location, in the Conwy valley near Llanrwst, it has by necessity evolved as a fortified residence.

For five hundred years from the time of the Battle of Llanrwst in 984 AD, this area was heavily contested in turn by the rulers of Gwynedd and Deheubarth, by Owain Glyndŵr's rebel army and by Dafydd ap Siencyn, who led a band of pro-Lancastrian fighters during the Wars of the Roses.

By the fifteenth century Gwydir belonged to Hywel Coetmor, one of Glyndŵr's commanders. At the end of the century it was bought and rebuilt by Welsh nobleman Maredudd ab Ifan ab Robert, who founded the Wynn dynasty.

The Wynns remained at Gwydir until the late seventeenth century, refurbishing and enlarging the castle and gardens and adding a four-storey solar tower in the early to mid-sixteenth century.

Gwydir was then bought by the Willoughby de Eresby family as a summer residence. After two fires the castle had fallen into dereliction by the 1920s, and despite some restoration work from the 1940s by the Clegg family it was again derelict.

In 1994 the castle was purchased by artist Peter Welford and his wife Judy Corbett, who set about restoring it to its former glory, re-acquiring furnishings that had once belonged to the castle, such as the dining room bought by American newspaper magnate William Randolph Hearst.

··

Pages 36-37: Gwydir Castle is regarded as one of the finest Tudor houses in Wales.
Pages 38-39: The Castle's historic gardens are one of a very small number in Wales to have received Grade 1 listed status.

Penrhyn Castle

Bangor, Gwynedd, LL57 4HN.
Constructed 1819-1837.
www.nationaltrust.org.uk.

···

Penrhyn Castle, near Bangor in Gwynedd, shares the Norman style but not the long military history of other castles of that era in Wales.

The castle was built in the early nineteenth century on the site of a fortified manor house on an estate once owned by the twelfth-century Welsh nobleman Ednyfed Fychan, an ancestor of the Tudor dynasty. It was designed by the English architect Thomas Hopper for George Hay Dawkins-Pennant, who inherited the estate from his cousin Richard Pennant, owner of the Penrhyn slate quarry at Bethesda.

The Pennant fortune also stemmed from Caribbean sugar plantations which took advantage of slave labour, and Pennant and Dawkins-Pennant opposed the abolition of slavery and the emancipation of slaves in Parliament.

Construction of Penrhyn Castle began in 1819 and was completed just a few years before Dawkins-Pennant's death in 1840, when ownership passed to Edward Douglas-Pennant.

In October 1859 the *North Wales Chronicle* reported on Queen Victoria and Prince Albert's three-day stay at the castle, for which occasion the Douglas-Pennants had commissioned a one-tonne slate four-poster bed.

By the turn of the twentieth century both castle and quarry belonged to George Douglas-Pennant, who became involved in a bitter dispute with his quarry workers that led to a long and damaging strike between 1900-03.

During the London Blitz of World War Two paintings were evacuated from the National Gallery to Penrhyn Castle for safekeeping. Since 1951 Penrhyn has been in the care of the National Trust.

....

Pages 40-41: The gatehouse at Penrhyn Castle.
Pages 42-43: The castle was constructed to a neo-Norman design by architect Thomas Hopper (1776-1856).

Rhuddlan Castle

Castle Street, Rhuddlan, Denbighshire,
LL18 5AD.
Constructed 1277-1282.
www.cadw.wales.gov.uk.

••

**The concentric castle of Rhuddlan, set
inland from the north Wales coastline on
the River Clwyd, was built as the centre of
operations for King Edward I's campaign
against the native Prince of Wales,
Llywelyn ap Gruffudd.**

Construction began in 1277 and lasted
for five years, with its completion overseen
by the king's castle builder, James of
St George. The inner ring of the castle was
designed in a diamond shape, guarded
by two double and two single towers.
To ensure supply by sea, the river leading
to the castle was deepened and widened.

Edward I settled at the castle, and
Queen Eleanor of Castile gave birth to
their daughter Elizabeth here in 1282.
In 1284 the castle lent its name to the
Statute of Rhuddlan, a proclamation
in which the king set out his plans for
governing Wales.

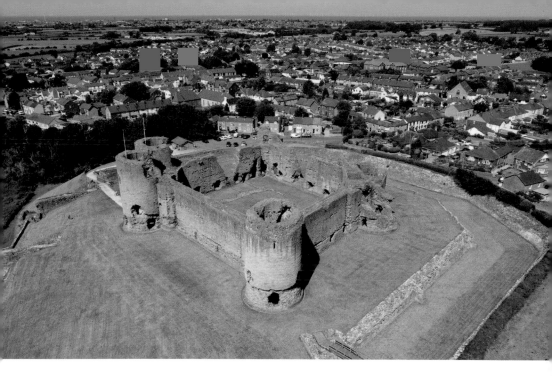

Controversially, these included the creation of his own non-native Prince of Wales. The statute survived until the 1530s.

Rhuddlan Castle survived attacks during Welsh uprisings led by Madog ap Llywelyn in 1294 and Owain Glyndŵr in 1400. During the English Civil War the castle's garrison was Royalist, but in 1646 il was captured by Parliamentarians and slighted on the orders of Oliver Cromwell.

Pages 44-45: Rhuddlan Castle overlooking the River Clwyd.
Page 46: The west gatehouse, composed of two concentric towers.
Page 47: An aerial view of the castle.

Mid Wales
Aberystwyth Castle

New Promenade, Aberystwyth, Ceredigion, SY23 2AU.
Constructed 1277-1289.
www.aberystwyth.gov.uk.

....

Aberystwyth, on the mid Wales coastline, was the site of an early twelfth-century fortress that was bitterly contested for more than 150 years by the Welsh and their Norman invaders. When King Edward I commissioned the construction of a stone castle in 1277, however, a different site a mile further north was chosen, on a promontory overlooking Cardigan Bay.

Work was temporarily interrupted in 1282 when the castle was captured and burned by an army led by Dafydd ap Gruffudd, brother of Llywelyn. After being won back by the English, it was completed in grand style in 1289 with the help of James of St George, architect of Edward I's 'Iron Ring' of castles around north Wales.

The castle's coastal location helped it to withstand a prolonged siege during Madog ap Llywelyn's revolt of 1294, but in 1404, during the Owain Glyndŵr uprising, it fell to a Welsh force who also blockaded it by sea.

Henry of Monmouth, later King Henry V, recaptured the castle in 1208, but it slowly lost its strategic value and fell into disrepair.

In 1637 a royal mint was established at Aberystwyth Castle by King Charles I which turned out silver shillings from a local mine. During the English Civil War the mint was guarded by a regiment of Royalist soldiers, bringing it into the sights of the Parliamentarians. Oliver Cromwell ordered its capture in 1646 and its destruction three years later, quite possibly using gunpowder stored there for use in mining work.

....

Page 48: The remains of the north gate at Aberystwyth Castle.

Brecon Castle

Castle Square, Brecon, Powys, LD3 9DB.
Constructed 11th-12th century.
www.breconcastle.co.uk.

Brecon Castle, on a hillside above the meeting of the rivers Honddu and Usk, dates back to the first Norman invasion of Wales. Work on an earth and timber stronghold here began under Bernard de Neufmarché, whose conquest of the Welsh kingdom of Brycheiniog was sealed at the Battle of Brecon in 1093.

Reinforced in stone, the castle came under repeated attack from Welsh forces between 1215-1276, regularly changing hands until the Crown took ownership in the late fourteenth century.

Brecon Castle was besieged by Parliamentarians during the English Civil War and fell into decline until the early nineteenth century, when part of it was restored and incorporated into a hotel by the Morgan family of Tredegar Park, near Newport.

Pages 50-51: Brecon Castle sits above the confluence of the Rivers Honddu and Usk.

Chirk Castle

Chirk, Wrexham, LL14 5AF.
Constructed 1295-1310.
www.nationaltrust.org.uk.

....

Chirk Castle, overlooking the Ceiriog Valley to the south-west of Wrexham, was built at the turn of the fourteenth century in the style of King Edward I's master mason, James of St George. Chirk is an 'Iron Ring' castle in miniature, however, with its round towers and curtain walls less developed than those in Beaumaris or Harlech.

The castle was raised by Roger Mortimer, who had supported Edward I's conquest of Wales in 1282, and in return was granted a Marcher lordship: a title and a stretch of land to protect along the Welsh border.

He and other early owners of Chirk Castle shared a colourful history, with Mortimer losing the castle when he was imprisoned in the Tower of London in 1322 for rebelling against King Edward II. He died in the Tower four years later.

In 1334 the castle was handed to Richard FitzAlan, Earl of Arundel, who also contrived to lose it through treason, this time against King Richard II. FitzAlan was executed in 1397.

His son, Thomas FitzAlan, fared better with his treasonous behaviour, regaining his family estates after helping Henry Bolingbroke to overthrow Richard II and assume the throne as King Henry IV in 1399.

In the fifteenth century Chirk Castle was acquired by Sir William Stanley, another nobleman with a taste for insurrection. Stanley played a prominent role in King Richard III's defeat at the Battle of Bosworth

in 1485, which allowed Henry Tudor to become king, but Stanley later incurred Henry's wrath by supporting another claim to the throne and was executed in 1495.

In 1595 the castle was bought by Sir Thomas Myddelton I, an early investor in the East India Company and Lord Mayor of London from 1613-16. Sir Thomas converted the castle into a stately mansion and in 1630 performed an important service for Welsh culture by helping to publish 500 copies of a portable Welsh translation of the Bible. Badly damaged during the Civil War, when the twelve-year-old Sir Thomas Myddelton III inherited the castle in 1663, his grandmother, Mary Napier, supervised its repair.

As the castle continued to pass down through the Myddelton family, its gardens were landscaped by William Emes in the eighteenth century and in 1845 the castle's interior was redesigned by Gothic revivalist architect A.W.N. Pugin.

In 1910 Chirk Castle was leased to Thomas Scott-Ellis, a patron of the arts, playwright and librettist who modernised it before leaving in 1946. The Myddeltons still live at the castle, which has been in the care of the National Trust since 1981.

··

Pages 52-53: Chirk Castle from the gardens.
Page 54: Restored statue of Hercules in the castle grounds.
Page 55: A lavish 17th-century interior.

Harlech Castle

Castle Square, Harlech, LL46 2YH.
Constructed 1282-1286.
UNESCO World Heritage Site.
www.cadw.wales.gov.uk.

....

One of King Edward I's 'Iron Ring' of castles around north Wales, Harlech Castle sits imperiously on a high stone spur looking out over Tremadog Bay in Ardudwy, Gwynedd.

According to the *Mabinogion*, the medieval collection of ancient oral Welsh mythology and folklore, this same spur was once the site of the court of the giant King Bendigeidfran, or Brân the Blessed, who according to legend waded across the Irish Sea to rescue his sister Branwen from the Irish King Matholwch.

Construction of the castle as it looks today began in 1283 after the death of Llywelyn ap Gruffudd as King Edward I sought to push into Gwynedd to complete his conquest of Wales.

Symmetrical and concentric, with a circular tower at each corner and an imposing gatehouse on the eastern side, the castle took seven years to complete under the supervision of Edward I's master mason, James of St George.

During the Welsh insurgency of Madog ap Llywelyn in 1294-5 the castle was besieged but held out as supplies delivered by sea were smuggled from a small harbour up a stone staircase and into the castle. After the siege Harlech

Harlech Castle became Glyndŵr's headquarters and personal residence until, in 1408, it was besieged by English forces led by Henry of Monmouth, later King Henry V. When the castle fell in 1409, Glyndŵr escaped, but his wife, Margaret Hanmer, and some of their children and grandchildren were captured and imprisoned in the Tower of London.

In contrast, after Lancastrian King Henry VI was seized by Yorkists at the Battle of Northampton in 1460 during the lengthy Wars of the Roses, his wife, Queen Margaret, fled to the safety of Harlech Castle.

A year later, King Edward IV ordered his troops into Wales. As castle after castle fell to the Yorkists, Harlech alone stood strong until 1468 when, after a prolonged siege, it fell to an army led by William Herbert, first Earl of Pembroke. The resistance of the castle's Lancastrian garrison is said to have inspired the nineteenth-century song 'Men of Harlech'.

Castle's defences were strengthened, and again in the 1320s, but these reinforcements were not enough to prevent it from being overrun by Owain Glyndŵr's army in 1404.

Damaged in the siege, Harlech Castle fell into disrepair until the English Civil War, when it was garrisoned and repaired by Royalists under the charge of Colonel William Owen in 1642. Another siege followed in 1646 and in yet another campaign the castle became the last stronghold to fall, this time to the Parliamentarians. Orders to destroy the castle were never fully carried out, but in due course the castle was abandoned.

The ruins, remarkably intact, proved a popular attraction for artists and sightseers in the eighteenth and nineteenth centuries. After World War One the Crown's Office of Works carried out some restoration work on the site. In 1986 Harlech Castle was listed, alongside three more of Edward I's north Wales castles, as a UNESCO World Heritage Site.

Pages 56-57: Harlech Castle looking towards Snowdonia.
Pages 58-59: The main castle entrance.
Pages 60-61: View of the gatehouse and inner ward.

Powis Castle
and Garden

Welshpool, Powys, SY21 8RF.
Constructed 13th century.
www.nationaltrust.org.uk.

An elegant red stone fortress-turned-mansion house which rises above a series of terraced gardens near Welshpool in Powys, Powis Castle was originally a Welsh castle. The first stronghold on the site belonged to Owain Cyfeiliog, a twelfth-century prince of Powys. It was passed down through the family to his grandson, Gruffudd ap Gwenwynwyn, an enemy of the princes of Gwynedd and a supporter of the Crown.

After Powis was attacked and largely destroyed in 1274 by Llywelyn ap Gruffudd, ruler of Gwynedd and Prince of Wales, Gruffudd ap Gwenwynwyn was forced into exile in Shrewsbury. The pair's fates were swiftly reversed, however. Gruffudd ap Gwenwynwyn sided with King Edward I's conquest of Wales from 1277, and so reclaimed and rebuilt his castle in stone a few years later. Llywelyn was killed in battle in 1282.

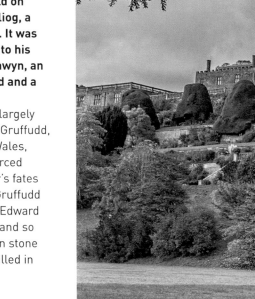

By the sixteenth century Powis Castle had fallen on hard times. In the 1530s it was acquired by Sir Edward Grey, who began to restore it. In 1587 Grey sold the castle to Sir Edward Herbert, beginning a long association with the family which continues today. The Herberts transformed Powis Castle into an extravagant country house, adding an ornate Elizabethan Long Gallery, now home to a collection of twelve seventeenth-century busts of the Roman Caesars.

More modifications were carried out after 1784 when the castle passed by marriage into the hands of Edward Clive, son of Major-General Robert Clive, an agent of the East India Company dubbed 'Clive of India' for helping to establish British rule on the subcontinent.

Edward Clive served as Governor of Madras from 1798-1804 and returned home with a collection of South Asian artefacts, some acquired by his father, which have formed the basis of the Clive Museum at Powis Castle since 1987.

Further improvements were made to the castle in the early twentieth century by George Herbert, fourth Earl of Powis, and his wife Violet. The countess turned her attention to restoring the castle's baroque seventeenth-century terraced gardens and added a new formal garden. The castle has been with the National Trust since 1952.

....

Pages 62-63: Powis Castle viewed from below.
Page 64: Statue of Fame in the entrance courtyard.
Page 65: The castle interior.
Pages 66-67: Aerial view of the terraced gardens and castle.

Tretower Court and Castle

Tretower, Crickhowell, Powys, NP8 1RD.
Constructed 12th century.
www.cadw.wales.gov.uk.

....

A mile north of the River Usk, near Crickhowell in Powys, the tall, circular tower of a Norman castle stands adjacent to a stately fortified medieval house.

Tretower Castle was built on the site of an earlier motte and bailey fort by the Picard family, Norman invaders, from 1150. It resisted attack during both the 1233 uprising by Richard Marshal, the third Earl of Pembroke, and Owain Glyndŵr's revolt of 1400-1415.

Tretower Court emerged during the fifteenth century under the ownership of Sir Roger Vaughan, who fought at Agincourt in 1415 alongside his father, who was killed.

The Vaughans left Tretower in the 1780s and the court was used as a farm building before coming under the care of Cadw.

....

Pages 68-69: The circular tower is the main remnant of Tretower Castle.

South Wales
Caerphilly Castle

Castle Street, Caerphilly, CF83 1JD.
Constructed 1268-1290.
www.cadw.wales.gov.uk.

....

Caerphilly is a castle of superlatives. Spanning more than 120,000 square metres, it is the largest medieval castle in Wales. (Across Britain, according to Cadw, the Welsh Government's historic environment service, only Windsor Castle is larger.) With its twin rings of curtain wall, Caerphilly Castle was also the first concentric fortification in Wales.

It was built from 1268 by Gilbert de Clare, seventh Earl of Gloucester and the Marcher Lord of Glamorgan, to meet the growing threat posed by Llywelyn ap Gruffudd, acknowledged by King Henry III as the Prince of Wales just a decade earlier.

In 1270 Llywelyn tried to destroy the castle, but Gilbert prevailed, and when construction was completed in 1290, at the cost of £19,000, the castle boasted an imposing pair of twin-towered gatehouses, a 20m-tall cylindrical tower at each corner and was surrounded by water defences.

Caerphilly was again attacked during Madog ap Llywelyn's 1294-5 uprising by a force led by Morgan ap Maredudd, whose family estates had been taken by Gilbert de Clare, but the attack failed. Gilbert died a year later, leaving the castle to his wife, Joan of Acre, daughter of King Edward I, and their son, also Gilbert. After the latter's death at Bannockburn in 1314, 'Llywelyn Bren' ('Llywelyn of the Woods') laid siege to the castle and succeeded in breaking through its first line of defences before being driven off by an army hastily sent forth by King Edward II.

The castle passed to Joan's daughter, Eleanor de Clare, and its ornate great hall was remodelled by her husband, Hugh Despenser the Younger, a close adviser to Edward II, who was executed in a grisly fashion for treason in 1326.

Caerphilly Castle survived the Glyndŵr uprising but began to deteriorate from the end of the fifteenth century.

The slide was halted in the 1870s when it was acquired by John Crichton-Stuart, third Marquess of Bute, who added a grand wooden roof to the great hall. Restoration continued in the twentieth century under the fourth marquess and the castle was gifted to the state by the fifth marquess in 1950.

Pages 70-71: Caerphilly is the largest medieval castle in Wales.
Pages 72-73: The castle's main entrance.
Page 74: An aerial view showing the series of surrounding moats.
Page 75: The roof of the great hall was restored during the 20th century.

Caldicot Castle

Church Road, Caldicot, Monmouthshire,
NP26 4HU.
Constructed 11th-13th century.
www.visitwales.com.

....

**Although the stonework of Caldicot Castle
dates back to the medieval era, the strategic
importance of its location, near to the mouth
of the River Severn above the Gwent Levels
in Monmouthshire, suggests that earlier
strongholds would have existed here too.**

The castle overlooks the River Nedern, not
far from the old Roman settlement of Venta
Silurum at Caerwent and an Anglo-Saxon
hunting lodge at Portskewett belonging to
Harold Godwinson, later King Harold II.

It is believed a Norman motte and bailey
fort occupied the site of the present castle
towards the end of the eleventh century.
The fort was strengthened during the early
twelfth century by Walter FitzRoger, the
Anglo-Norman sheriff of Gloucester, and
his son, Miles FitzWalter, the first Earl of
Hereford.

In the mid-twelfth century the castle
passed by marriage into the hands of the
prominent nobleman Humphrey II de Bohun.

His heir, Humphrey III de Bohun, was appointed Lord High Constable of England by King Henry II in 1164, a role that was held by the next seven generations of the de Bohun family.

Much of the castle's stone fortifications, in the form of a keep and a curtain wall, were built over a fifty-year period from 1221. A great hall, originally built in wood, was added in the 1340s.

The long custodianship of the de Bohuns ended towards the end of the fourteenth century, when the castle passed again by marriage to Thomas of Woodstock, youngest child of King Henry III and an uncle to King Richard II.

Woodstock ordered further building work in the 1380s including new accommodation within the three-storey Woodstock Tower, which bears the inscriptions of his name and that of his wife, Alianore. Woodstock died in 1397 awaiting trial for treason after plotting to overthrow his nephew the king, and Caldicot became part of the Duchy of Lancaster. The castle was owned by King Henry V in the fifteenth century and slighted during the 1640s following the English Civil War.

Towards the end of the nineteenth century the site was bought by J. R. Cobb, a lawyer and castle enthusiast who had carried out restoration projects at Pembroke and Manorbier castles from the 1880s. Cobb died in 1897 having begun work on his dream of restoring Caldicot Castle as his own domestic residence, and the work was seen through over a period of twenty years by his son, Geoffrey Wheatley Cobb. The gatehouse was transformed into living quarters and some of the towers, including the Woodstock Tower, were refurbished as rental accommodation. A cannon belonging to the HMS *Foudroyant*, once Admiral Horatio Nelson's flagship, was installed within the grounds after the ship was bought by the family. The Cobbs continued to live at the castle until 1963 when it was sold to Chepstow Rural District Council. The castle and its 55-acre gardens have since remained in the possession of the local authority and are open to the public.

Pages 76-77: Aerial view of Caldicot Castle.
Page 79: The drawbridge and main gate.

Cardiff Castle

Castle Street, Cardiff, CF10 3RB.
Constructed c. 11th century, with later additions.
www.cardiffcastle.com.

....

Standing in parkland in the heart of what is now the capital city of Wales, Cardiff Castle has served as a wartime defensive shield for almost 2,000 years.

In the first century AD, an earth and timber fort on this site provided sanctuary for Roman legionaries garrisoned to protect a key stretch of the road between settlements at Caerwent and Carmarthen from the Silures, a warlike Celtic tribe.

During the Blitz of the 1940s, tunnels were dug underground within the walls of what was by then an ancient medieval castle to offer nightly shelter to 1,800 inhabitants of the major coal port seeking safety from the Luftwaffe's incendiaries.

Four Roman forts were built on the site over a period of 300 years, with the stone walls of the last remaining undiscovered until 1888. Soon after the Norman invasion in 1066, a motte and bailey fortress was built on the last of these Roman forts, from which Robert Fitzhamon, a cousin and ally of William the Conqueror, ruled over Glamorgan. From the 1260s, with the Anglo-Normans and Welsh still battling for control, Fitzhamon's fortress was reinforced in stone by Gilbert de Clare, who was also responsible for building Caerphilly Castle.

In the early fourteenth century both Cardiff and Caerphilly castles passed to the Despenser family, who in 1317 executed 'Llywelyn Bren' ('Llywelyn of the Woods'), a nobleman who had led a revolt the previous year.

Llywelyn's death was lamented by the Welsh and was likely on the mind of Owain Glyndŵr when he stormed the castle in 1404, set fire to it and routed the town that had grown up around it.

After Glyndŵr's defeat the castle passed to the Beauchamp family, who built new lodgings along the west wall. William Herbert, guardian of the young King Edward VI, took possession in 1551 and it was further expanded.

The castle was besieged and taken by the Parliamentarians in the English Civil War. Though damaged during the fighting, unlike many other Welsh castles it was not purposely slighted.

From 1776 until 1947, when it was gifted to the local council, Cardiff Castle was owned by the Bute family. During the 1770s landscaper Lancelot 'Capability' Brown and architect Henry Holland redesigned its gardens and accommodation. Brown's efforts included clearing away the lodgings of the Norman knights and the shire hall from the green, stripping the keep of its ivy, removing the trees from the ancient mound and filling in the moat, while Holland partitioned the great hall off into a new entrance hall, library and dining room, among other remodelling and reconstruction.

Some further restoration work took place during the 1820s under the second Marquess of Bute, who based himself at Cardiff Castle during the events of the 1831 Merthyr Rising and led the government response. The next significant period of change for the site would not come until 1865, however, when the third Marquess, John Crichton-Stuart, having come of age and inherited his father's estate, began a sixteen-year creative partnership with the architect William Burges, during which the castle was transformed into a Gothic-style medieval fortified mansion.

Among a series of ornate rooms designed by Burges, the Arab Room in the Herbert Tower, built up from a sixteenth-century wing, boasts an elaborate Moorish ceiling hand-decorated in valuable gold leaf, marbled floors and walls, cedar wood cabinets inlaid with silver and statuettes of eastern deities. Considered to be among the most significant Victorian interiors in Britain, this was the last room Bruges worked on before falling ill, his death coming in April 1881. Bute memorialised the architect by placing Bruges's initials, together with his own and the date, into the fireplace of the Arab Room.

After Burges's death, his former assistant William Frame continued his work, which included a wall featuring a menagerie of stone-sculptured animals, restoring the newly discovered Roman remains and the completion of the clock tower on the site of a Roman bastion in 1885.

Following the handover of the castle to the city in 1947 the main range hosted the Royal Welsh College of Music and Drama from its founding in 1949 until relocation in 1998. A new interpretation centre opened alongside the South Gate at a cost of £6 million in 2008 and the castle is today used for a range of cultural and social events.

Page 80: Cardiff Castle from Bute Park.
Pages 82-83: The 19th-century palace in the Gothic Revival style by architect William Burges.
Pages 84-85: The Banqueting Hall, Cardiff Castle.
Page 86: Ceiling of the Arab Room, Cardiff Castle.
Page 87 The Norman keep.

Castell Coch

Tongwynlais, Cardiff, CF15 7JS.
Constructed 13th century.
Rebuilt 1875-1891.
www.cadw.wales.gov.uk.

••

In the 1870s, after starting their Gothic revival of Cardiff Castle, John Crichton-Stuart, third Marquess of Bute, and the renowned Victorian architect William

Burges turned their attention north of the city to the remains of a thirteenth-century fortress dominating the entrance to the Taff Valley, near Tongwynlais.

The first stronghold here was a wood and earth fort, built in the late eleventh century to consolidate Norman gains in the area. In the 1260s, when the lordship of Glamorgan passed to Gilbert de Clare, he set about rebuilding the fort. His castle took its name, Castell Coch, or Red Castle,

not from the colour of Gilbert's hair, which earned him the nickname 'the Red Earl', but from the shade of its sandstone.

Gilbert died in 1295, and his son, also named Gilbert, was killed at Bannockburn in 1314. Two years later Castell Coch was attacked by Welsh rebels led by 'Llywelyn Bren' ('Llywelyn of the Woods'). It was significantly damaged and fell out of use.

Crichton-Stuart's excavation of the ruins began in 1871 and in 1875 Burges began transforming them into a French-styled fantasy castle complete with conical towers and ornate and colourful interiors, including the gilded octagonal drawing room.

Page 88: The keep, gatehouse and well tower.
Page 89: The inner courtyard.
Page 90: The highly decorated interior.
Page 91: Overlooking the River Taf.

Chepstow Castle

Bridge Street, Chepstow, Monmouthshire, NP16 5EY.
Constructed 11th century.
www.cadw.wales.gov.uk.

....

Wood-dating techniques have revealed that the vast oak doors of Chepstow Castle were fashioned before 1190, which, according to the Welsh Government's historic environment service, Cadw, makes them the oldest castle doors in Europe.

The castle itself, standing dramatically upon a vertical limestone cliff above the River Wye in Monmouthshire, is mentioned in Britain's oldest public record, the Domesday Book of 1086. Chepstow was Wales's first stone castle and predates its ornate doors by more than a century.

William FitzOsbern, a close confidant of William the Conqueror, is credited with starting construction work in 1067. FitzOsbern died just four years later, and it is thought the castle's great stone tower, completed in 1090, may have been the work of King William I himself, who visited Chepstow in 1081.

The next major building phase, which coincides with the origins of the castle's doors, began in around 1189 after both

Chepstow and Pembroke castles had been granted to William Marshal, Earl of Pembroke. A celebrated soldier, Marshal would later serve as Protector of the Realm for the young King Henry III. He also negotiated the signing of the Magna Carta, of which he himself was a signatory. In the thirty years until his death in 1219 a new gatehouse and tower were added and the castle's defences were significantly strengthened.

In the mid-thirteenth century Chepstow Castle passed to Roger Bigod, Earl of Norfolk, who refurbished its living quarters and built the tower later named after Henry Marten, a signatory of King Charles I's death warrant in 1649.

Strongly garrisoned, the castle avoided attack during Owain Glyndŵr's rebellion, but during the English Civil War it was besieged twice, in 1645 and 1648, before falling to Parliamentarian forces who briefly used it as a prison before slighting it.

In 1914 the castle ruins were bought and partially restored by steel manufacturer William Royse Lysaght before they were entrusted to the government in the 1950s.

....

Pages 92-93: Chepstow Castle is imposingly positioned on a limestone cliff above the River Wye.
Pages 94-95: Marten's Tower (left), built by Roger Bigod, fifth Earl of Norfolk, between 1288-1293, and the gatehouse (right).

Monmouth Castle

Monmouth, Monmouthsire, NP25 3BS.
Constructed 11th-12th century.
www.cadw.wales.gov.uk.

··

Historians disagree on exactly when Monmouth Castle became the birthplace of one of England's great warrior kings – 1386 or 1387 – but few argue over his greatest achievement. King Henry V's victory over a superior French force at Agincourt in 1415, aided by 500 Welsh longbowmen, was immortalised by Shakespeare.

The first ringwork defences rose at Monmouth in the mid-eleventh century under William FitzOsbern, confidant of William the Conqueror and a key figure in the Norman Conquest. Fortified in stone in the 1120s, the addition of a great hall, a tower, a town wall and a fortified bridge brought Monmouth Castle to royal prominence before it was slighted on the orders of Oliver Cromwell, who visited during the English Civil War.

··

Pages 96-97: Only the ruins of the Great Tower and hall remain of Monmouth Castle.

Ogmore Castle

Bridgend, CF32 0QP.
Constructed c. 12th century.
www.cadw.wales.gov.uk.

The ruins of Ogmore Castle lie in green fields alongside the River Ewenny, close to where it flows into the Ogmore Estuary, near Bridgend.

The fortress was founded in 1106 by William de Londres, one of twelve knights who helped Norman lord Robert Fitzhamon conquer the kingdom of Morgannwg, and was strengthened in stone during the thirteenth century before passing from the de Londres family to the Duchy of Lancaster in 1298. The castle was damaged during Owain Glyndŵr's rebellion in 1405 and fell into disrepair after the sixteenth century.

A chain of stepping stones dating back to medieval times leads across the River Ewenny from the castle to the floodplain on the other side and is a popular local landmark.

Pages 98-99: Stepping stones span the River Ewenny below the ruin of Ogmore Castle.

Raglan Castle

Castle Road, Raglan, Monmouthsire,
NP15 2BT.
Constructed c. 15th century.
www.cadw.wales.gov.uk.

The colourful family of Welsh nobleman and soldier Sir William ap Thomas were the driving force behind the transformation of Raglan Castle, near Abergavenny in Monmouthshire, into one of the most impressive in Wales.

Sir William, known as 'the Blue Knight of Gwent' after the shade of his armour, began construction in the 1430s on the site of an eleventh-century Norman motte and bailey fort.

Raglan, one of Britain's last medieval castles, was intended to be as lavish a mansion house as it was a fortress. Its pale Great Tower, known as the 'Yellow Tower of Gwent', was surrounded by a moat and could only be approached from within the castle.

On Sir William's death in 1445 his son, William Herbert, known as 'Gwilym Ddu' ('Black William'), added further adornments and a gatehouse to the castle before his death in 1469.

From the sixteenth century William Somerset, third Earl of Worcester, and his heirs created a long gallery and elaborate Renaissance gardens.

It was Raglan's allegiance to the Crown that brought about its downfall. After a ten-week siege and heavy bombardment by Parliamentarian forces during the English Civil War in 1646 the castle was surrendered and then deliberately slighted.

Pages 100-101: The main gatehouse at Raglan Castle.
Page 102: The remains of the Great Tower and moat.
Page 103: Front view of the Great Tower, also known as the Yellow Tower of Gwent, one of Raglan's most striking features.

St Donat's Castle

St Donat's, Llantwit Major,
Vale of Glamorgan, CF61 1YZ.
Constructed c. 12th century.
www.uwcatlanticexperience.com.

···

St Donat's Castle, near Llantwit Major on the Vale of Glamorgan coastline, has been occupied since the twelfth century. It is thought the site was home to the first-century British chieftain Caradog (Caratacus), who fought to defend Britain from the Romans, and it is likely that a Norman-era wood and earth fort stood on the same spot.

The first stone fortifications were put up by the de Hawey/Stradling family around the turn of the thirteenth century, and by the sixteenth century the castle boasted two concentric curtain walls, an inner and outer gatehouse, a great hall, a series of courtyard buildings, terraced Tudor gardens and a cavalry barracks.

After supporting King Charles I during the English Civil War the Stradling family's fortunes began to wane. When Sir Thomas Stradling, the sixth baronet, was killed in a duel in 1738 the line ended and St Donat's passed out of the family after more than 400 years. Sir John Tyrwhitt acquired the estate in 1755 but after his death five years later it was allowed to fall into disrepair. In 1862 St Donat's was bought by a descendant of the Stradlings, Dr John

Nicholl Carne, who set about restoring it. Restoration work was continued by Morgan Stuart Williams, from a mine-owning family in Aberpergwm, Neath, who took over the castle in 1901. After four years in the hands of the American diplomat Richard Pennoyer, in 1925 the castle and its 122-acre estate came to the attention of US media tycoon William Randolph Hearst when it was featured in a magazine.

Hearst, who had taken over his father's newspaper the *San Francisco Examiner* in 1887 and subsequently built up America's largest newspaper and media empire, paid £27,000 for St Donat's and shelled out a further £280,000 for the renovation of what was just one of many grand properties that he owned.

The work was carried out under the supervision of Sir Charles Allom, the architect knighted for his work on Buckingham Palace in London, with fixtures and fittings sourced and imported from great houses and castles across Europe.

In the twelve years that Hearst owned St Donat's he and his mistress, actress Marion Davies, are estimated to have spent a total of just four months visiting, but during this time they hosted household names from the political world and from Hollywood. Winston Churchill, David Lloyd George and US Ambassador Joseph Kennedy were house guests, the latter with his son John, the future US President. Actors Charlie Chaplin, Douglas Fairbanks Jr, Errol Flynn and Clark Gable are also said to have attended lavish parties here.

The castle was put up for sale in 1937, finally being bought and gifted to a trust in 1960. Two years later the United World College of the Atlantic was founded here, the first college in a worldwide chain of educational establishments conceived by Dr Kurt Hahn, who set up Gordonstoun school in Scotland in 1934.

Pages 104-105: The main entrance to St Donat's Castle.
Page 106: The castle gatehouse.
Page 107: St Donat's now hosts the United World College of the Atlantic.

St Fagans Castle

Cardiff, CF5 6XB.
Constructed 16th century.
www.museum.wales.

....

The three-storey mansion at St Fagans, west of Cardiff, was built during the first Elizabethan era, but the site's historical significance can be traced back much further.

A ringwork fortress was erected on the site from 1091 by Peter le Sore on land granted to him by the Norman conqueror Robert Fitzhamon. A remnant of the thirteenth-century stone castle which superseded it is still visible in its forecourt.

In the fourteenth century the castle passed to the le Vele family, who sold it to lawyer Dr John Gibbon in 1563. The mansion and outer court as they exist today were built consecutively by Dr Gibbon, Sir Nicholas Herbert, who owned it from 1584, and Sir Edward Lewis, the owner from 1616.

In 1648, during the English Civil War, the fortified mansion emerged unscathed from the Battle of St Fagans, in which 11,000 men fought.

In the 1830s St Fagans passed to the Windsor-Clive family, who allowed their banqueting hall to be used as a convalescent hospital during World War One. In 1946 the castle was donated by Other Windsor-Clive, third Earl of Plymouth, to the National Museum of Wales and the open-air Welsh Folk Museum opened here in 1948.

Pages 108-109: The 16th-century Elizabethan manor house.
Page 110: The mansion was restored in the 1850s and presented to the National Museum of Wales in 1946.
Page 111: A view of one of the house's interiors.

West Wales
Carew Castle

Castle Lane, Carew, Tenby, Pembrokeshire, SA70 8SL.
Constructed c. 12th century.
www.pembrokeshirecoast.wales.

··

Half-castle, half-palace, the ruins of Carew look down over the tidal millpond of the River Carew, which leads via the River Daugleddau to the sea at Milford Haven in Pembrokeshire.

In the early twelfth century Gerald de Windsor, governor of Pembroke Castle, built his own fortress here on land owned by his wife Nest, daughter of Rhys ap Tewdwr, last king of Deheubarth.

Adopting the name de Carew on his death, Gerald's heirs enlarged on his work. In the thirteenth century, with the threat of Welsh rebellion, Sir Nicholas de Carew, a loyal soldier of King Edward I, rebuilt the castle in stone, creating inner and outer wards. By the end of the fifteenth century, however, the Carews had fallen on hard times.

In 1480 Sir Edmund Carew mortgaged the castle to Rhys ap Thomas, a prominent Welsh landholder who fought alongside Henry Tudor at the Battle of Bosworth in 1485 to take the throne from King Richard III. Richly rewarded by the new King Henry VII, Rhys turned Carew Castle into a lavish mansion, adding a gatehouse and embellishing the great hall.

In 1507, to celebrate being made a Knight of the Order of the Garter, Sir Rhys hosted a great tournament of arms in the meadows near the castle in which more than 600 noblemen did battle over a five-day period. Sir Rhys died in 1525, and in 1531 the castle passed into the hands of the Crown. In 1558 Queen Elizabeth I granted it to her lord deputy,

Sir John Perrot, who created a range of buildings on the north side of the castle with an Elizabethan-style façade.

In the seventeenth century, after a gap of more than a hundred years, ownership of the castle was returned to the Carew family, who have owned it ever since. Held originally by Royalists, Carew Castle changed hands three times during the English Civil War and fell into ruin after 1686.

....

Pages 112-113: The rear of Carew Castle, facing onto the River Carew.
Page 114: Aerial view over the castle.
Page 115: A view of the castle's walls and towers.

Carreg Cennen Castle

Trapp, Llandeilo, Carmarthenshire,
SA19 6UA.
Constructed c. 13th century.
www.cadw.wales.gov.uk.

....

It is said that Carreg Cennen Castle, built in a spectacular location above a limestone precipice on a hilltop near Llandeilo in Carmarthenshire, was once the site of a stronghold belonging to Urien Rheged, sixth-century Lord of Is-Cennen and one of King Arthur's knights, whose exploits were celebrated in the Book of Taliesin. Coins found there suggest the even earlier presence of the Romans.

The first castle at this site is attributed to Rhys ap Gruffudd, the Lord Rhys, the great warrior prince who fought to re-establish his ancestral kingdom of Deheubarth in the twelfth century. The castle was stormed by King Edward I's forces in 1277.

Though briefly held by the Welsh in 1282 under Llywelyn ap Gruffudd and in 1287 under Rhys ap Maredudd, from 1283 it belonged to John Giffard, an Anglo-Norman baron who demolished the Welsh-built structure and replaced it.

Towards the end of the fourteenth century Carreg Cennen passed to the Crown and so was contested by Owain Glyndŵr, who attacked with an army of 800 men in 1403. Glyndŵr's first assault was repelled by the castle's constable, John Scudamore, but he surrendered the much-damaged fortress after a siege.

The castle saw its last action during the Wars of the Roses. Garrisoned by Lancastrians, it was taken in 1462 by Yorkists, who then purposely slighted it. After centuries in ruins, some conservation work took place in the nineteenth century under John Frederick Vaughan Campbell, second Earl Cawdor, who was Member of Parliament for Pembrokeshire from 1841-60.

••

Pages 116-117: Carreg Cennen dominates the local skyline from its dramatic position. Pages 118-119: An aerial view over the ruins of the castle.

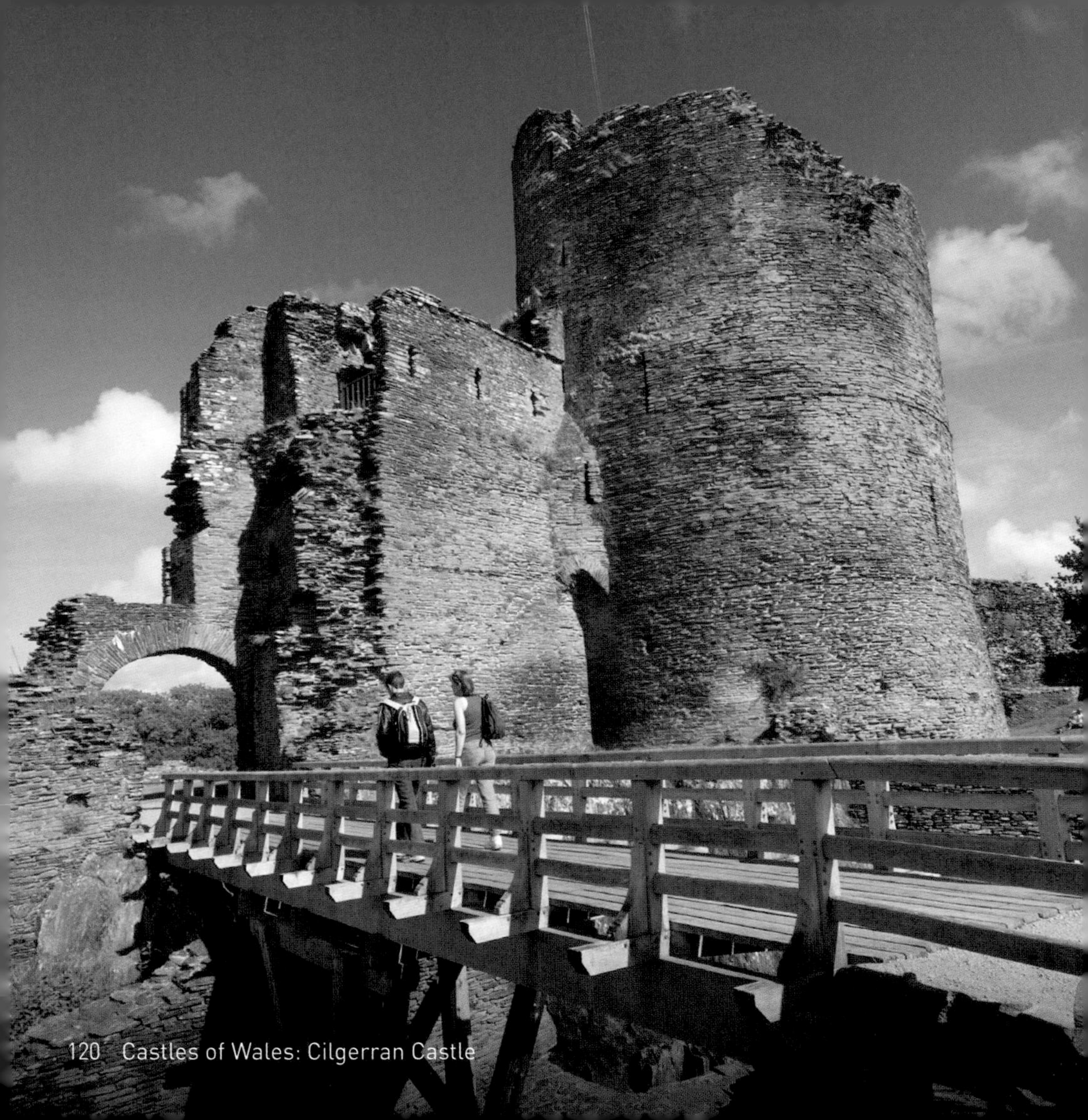

Cilgerran Castle

Castle Square, Cilgerran, Pembrokeshire,
SA43 2SF.
Constructed 13th century.
www.nationaltrust.org.uk.

The first castle built at Cilgerran, above the Teifi Gorge, near Cardigan in Ceredigion, dates back to the beginning of the twelfth century, when Norman lord Gerald de Windsor built a ringwork fortress, Cenarth Bychan, to protect his bride, Nest, the beautiful daughter of the last king of Deheubarth, Rhys ap Tewdwr.

Nest was nevertheless abducted from Cilgerran by her cousin, Owain ap Cadwgan, a prince of Powys, who had fallen in love with her. Nest had two children with Owain but Gerald won her back six years later, killing Owain in the process.

In 1165 Cilgerran was overrun by Rhys ap Gruffudd, the Lord Rhys, who then fought off two attacks by Anglo-Norman forces the following year. After the Lord Rhys's death in 1197, the Anglo-Norman warrior William Marshal, first Earl of Pembroke and later Protector of the Realm for the young King Henry III, succeeded in taking back Cilgerran in 1204.

Just eleven years later Cilgerran found itself in Welsh hands for the last time during the uprising led by Llywelyn ap Iorwerth, ruler of Gwynedd. Marshal's son, also William, regained the castle in 1223 and he set about constructing the stone walls and round towers whose remains are still visible today.

Cilgerran passed from the Marshal family in 1245 and during the revolt of Llywelyn ap Gruffudd came under the control of Prince Edward, later King Edward I. In 1258 a marauding Welsh force overcame an Anglo-Norman army near Cilgerran but failed to take and hold the castle.

By the early fourteenth century Cilgerran found itself in a dilapidated state but in 1377, fearing a French attack on the Welsh coast, King Edward III ordered the castle to be refortified. Cilgerran was badly damaged in 1405 during the Glyndŵr uprising, the last time the castle would see battle.

In the sixteenth century Cilgerran was gifted by King Henry VII to William Vaughan, sheriff of Cardiganshire, but the lordship was abolished by the 1536 Act of Union, marking the beginning of the castle's ultimate decline.

Cilgerran saw no action during the English Civil War, was abandoned and fell into ruins.

In 1863 slate quarrying close to the ruins caused a large chunk of masonry from the castle's wall to collapse. The damage was repaired after a campaign led by Henry J. Vincent, vicar of St Dogmaels.

During the 1920s the local council made efforts to make the ruins more presentable, and by 1928 entrance gates had been erected at the castle's two towers and the grounds cleared, reopening to the public in 1931. The ruins were registered as a Scheduled Ancient Monument in 1934.

In 1938 Cilgerran Castle was presented to the National Trust and a period of restoration work began, during which several important artefacts were uncovered, including four arrowheads in 1955 and coins dating back 500 and 700 years discovered during excavations in 1956.

Under the joint management of the National Trust and Cadw, the Welsh Government's historic environment service, the ruins were opened to visitors, with access to the castle made possible by a new wooden bridge over the drawbridge pit. Work was also carried out on a parapet walk linking the castle's east and west towers, reached through the east tower. In 2015 the castle was also the site of a reenactment of the Battle of Agincourt to mark the 600th anniversary.

Viewed from a distance in silhouette it is easy to see how Cilgerran Castle has inspired generations of artists. Perhaps the most notable among them has been Joseph Mallord William Turner, the great Romantic painter of light, who was drawn here in 1798 at the age of twenty-three and was sufficiently inspired to return again the following year, testing his technical skills to record the geography of north Wales in studies and material for later watercolours.

Turner followed in the footsteps of Richard Wilson, one of the founding members of the Royal Academy and an influential Welsh landscape artist, who painted the castle in 1773. In 2021 a

painting of Cilgerran Castle by Turner from the time of his visit in 1798 whose authenticity was subsequently dismissed for over a century, sold for £1m at auction in London.

Page 120: The west tower and gate to the inner ward at Cilgerran Castle.
Page 123: The inner courtyard.

Dinefwr Castle

Llandeilo, Carmarthenshire, SA19 6RT.
Constructed 12th century.
www.nationaltrust.org.uk.

The haunting, evocative ruins of Dinefwr Castle, near Llandeilo in Carmarthenshire, stand as a reminder of a great fortress which served as the court of one of the native princes of Wales.

Rhys ap Gruffudd, grandson of Rhys ap Tewdwr, the last king of Deheubarth, ruled over the kingdom for more than forty years from 1155, founding the castle on a rocky ridge above the River Tywi in the latter half of the twelfth century.

Rhys won back a large area of land in what is now mid and west Wales from the Norman invaders, effectively reconstituting Deheubarth, which he then sought to defend from attack by both Welsh and Anglo-Norman forces.

Following the accession of King Henry II in 1154, Rhys was forced to submit to the Crown, keeping Dinefwr but forsaking his princely title to become known as 'the Lord Rhys'.

The Lord Rhys oversaw a flourishing of Welsh culture and the bardic tournament he staged at Cardigan Castle in 1176 is recognised as the first eisteddfod ever to be held in Wales.

After his death in 1197 the kingdom of Deheubarth fell from grace and power. During the course of the next century Dinefwr Castle was repeatedly fought over and at one stage even partially demolished.

In 1287, a decade after King Edward I began his conquest of Wales, Dinefwr succumbed to Crown forces and was significantly reinforced. In 1403 the castle survived ten days under siege by an army led by Owain Glyndŵr.

At the end of the fifteenth century Dinefwr returned to family ownership under Rhys ap Thomas, a descendant of the Lord Rhys. He joined forces with Henry Tudor, who had landed at Milford Haven in 1485, shortly before the Battle of Bosworth, where some believe Rhys struck the blow that killed King Richard III.

Dinefwr Castle was part of his reward from a grateful King Henry VII, who installed him as Justiciar of Wales, a post also held by his tweltfth-century ancestor.

During the reign of the first Tudor king, Rhys ap Thomas carried out more building work on the castle before abandoning it in favour of the comforts of a new house nearby on the Dinefwr estate, on the site of what is now Newton House.

In 1531 Dinefwr was lost once again to the Crown when Rhys's grandson was beheaded for treason on the orders of a less grateful Tudor monarch, Henry VIII.

But ownership was restored to the family in the mid-seventeenth century in the form of Edward Rice, high sheriff of Carmarthenshire, who began redeveloping Newton House in 1660.

In 1775 the celebrated landscape gardener Lancelot 'Capability' Brown was commissioned by George Rice and his wealthy wife Cecil, née Talbot, to design the grounds at Dinefwr. Around this time the castle was fashioned into a romantic ruin and a summer house was installed on top of its keep.

Four stone turrets were added to Newton House in 1852, and in the 1960s, as its owner Richard Rhys sought to raise funds to maintain the house, Dinefwr once again became a home for art and culture, hosting a series of exhibitions and concerts.

However, in the mid-1970s the family was forced to sell up and the house fell into disrepair.

Dinefwr Castle was acquired by the Wildlife Trust of South and West Wales in 1979 and today is managed and maintained by Cadw, the Welsh Government's historic environment service. Cadw undertook a programme

of conservation beginning in 1982, including detailed surveys of upstanding masonry and the outlying earthworks, as well as further research into the medieval history of the site and partial reconstruction work.

Other parts of the estate at Dinefwr, including a deer park, were bought by the National Trust in 1987, with Newton House

also being taken into the Trust's care in 1990. Restoration work began in 1999 and the house was opened to the public.

Newton House is rumoured to be the most haunted National Trust house in Wales, containing a number of ghosts, including that of Lady Elinor Cavendish, who was murdered by a suitor in a top-floor nursery in the 1720s.

Page 124: The walls of the keep beside the castle entrance.
Pages 126-127: Walkways along the castle walls allow for views over the River Towy and the surrounding landscape.

Kidwelly Castle

Castle Road, Kidwelly, Carmarthenshire,
SA17 5BQ.
Constructed 12th century.
www.cadw.wales.gov.uk.

....

**Near the entrance to Kidwelly Castle,
on the Gwendraeth Estuary in
Carmarthenshire, stands a monument to
the only Welsh woman known to have led
a medieval Welsh army into battle.**

Gwenllian, wife of Gruffudd ap Rhys,
prince of Deheubarth, was thirty-six when
she was killed with one of her sons in a
battle here with the Norman lord Maurice
de Londres in 1136.

The first stronghold had been built on
the site by the Norman bishop Roger of
Salisbury twenty years earlier, and
de Londres had taken possession in the
1130s.

In the 1160s Kidwelly was captured and
held for seven years, perhaps in revenge,
by another of Gwenllian's sons, Rhys ap
Gruffudd, but it belonged mostly to the
de Londres family until 1216.

One of Wales's best-preserved castles, much of what stands today was built during the thirteenth century by the Chaworth and de Valence families. In the 1360s Kidwelly was acquired by John of Gaunt, son of King Edward III, but on his death in 1399 it reverted to the Crown and was further fortified.

The castle's concentric design proved crucial in repelling repeated attacks by Owain Glyndŵr's army between 1403-07, after which time Kidwelly Castle's importance waned.

....

Pages 128-129: Kidwelly Castle overlooking the River Gwendraeth.
Page 130: A view from below the castle walls.
Page 131: The gate towers at Kidwelly.

Laugharne Castle

King Street, Laugharne, Carmarthen,
SA33 4SA.
Constructed 13th century.
www.cadw.wales.gov.uk.

The once proud castle of Laugharne,
overlooking the Taf estuary in
Carmarthenshire, never recovered from
being slighted by Parliamentarians after
the English Civil War. This was not the
first time a stronghold here had been
demolished, however.

The first fortress was founded at Laugharne by the Anglo-Normans in the twelfth century. In 1171 King Henry II travelled to the castle to discuss a peace treaty with Rhys ap Gruffudd, ruler of Deheubarth.

On Henry II's death in 1189 the Lord Rhys seized the castle and burned it.

It was rebuilt and destroyed twice more by the native princes of Wales: in 1215 by Llywelyn ap Iorwerth, and then again in 1257 by Llywelyn ap Gruffudd.

The first stone fortifications were built by wealthy soldier-turned-admiral Guy de Brian and his family who owned the castle between 1247 and 1390.

By the mid-sixteenth century Laugharne Castle belonged to the Crown and in 1575 it was gifted by Queen Elizabeth I to Sir John Perrot, who she had commissioned to fight piracy in the waters off Pembrokeshire. Perrot converted the castle into a mansion and, after his death in the Tower of London while awaiting trial for treason in 1592, it was offered for rental.

Garrisoned by Royalists in 1644, Laugharne was besieged later that year and after a two-day artillery bombardment fell to a 2,000-strong Parliamentarian force led by the aptly named Major General Rowland Laugharne.

In 1730 another mansion, Castle House, was built nearby, leaving the ruins of Laugharne Castle to inspire notable artists and writers.

In 1831 J. M. W. Turner famously painted the castle amid a storm, while the poet Dylan Thomas, famed for writing in his nearby boathouse, today open to the public as a heritage centre, wrote his 1940 short story collection *Portrait of the Artist as a Young Dog* in a gazebo summerhouse built into the castle walls.

Page 133: Laugharne Castle from the Taf Estuary.
Page 134: The south-west tower and castle walls.
Page 135: Laugharne Castle in a storm by J. M. W. Turner, 1831.

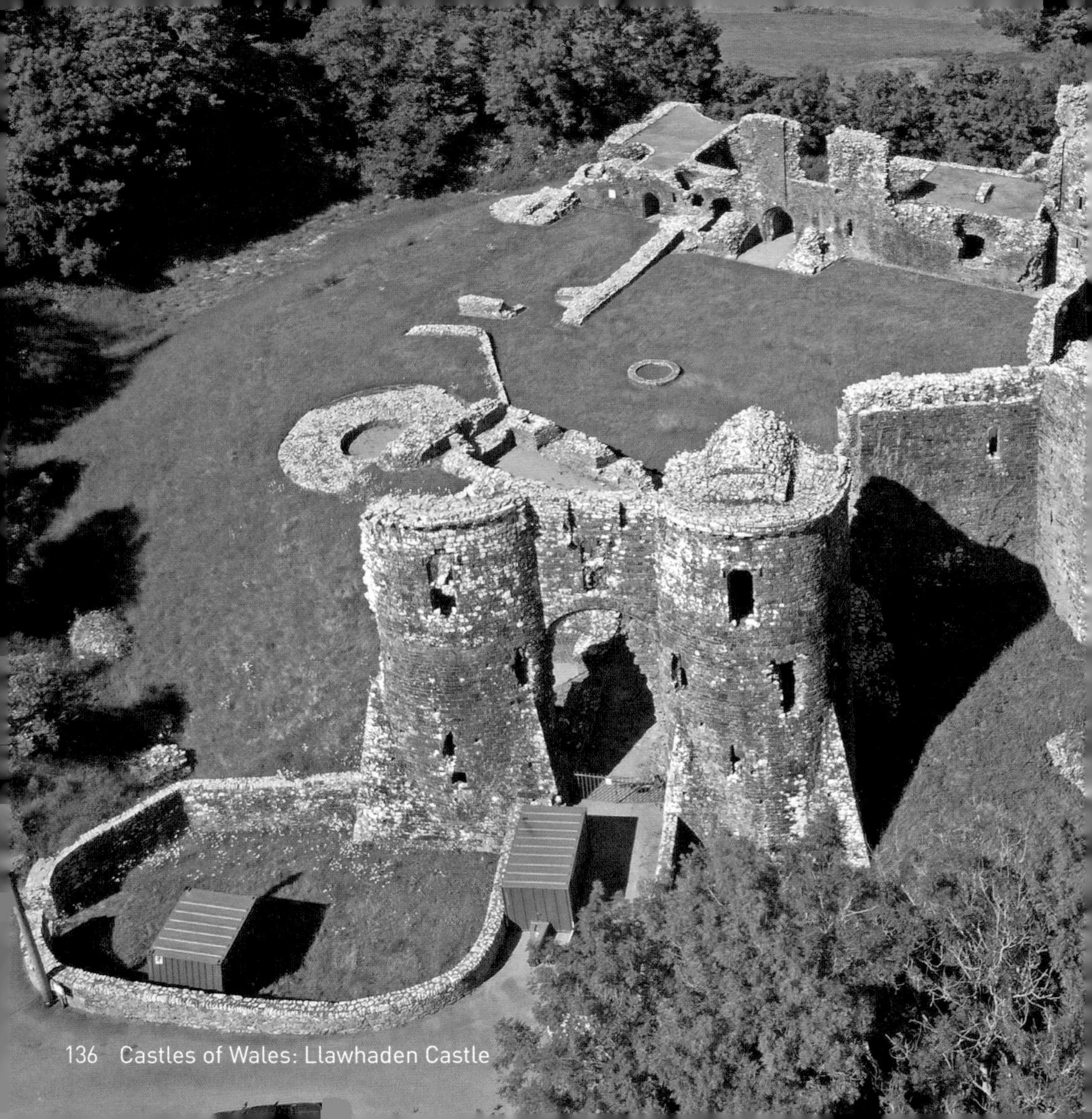

Llawhaden Castle

Tal-Y-Bont Hill, Llawhaden, Narberth,
SA67 8HL.
Constructed 13th-14th century.
www.cadw.wales.gov.uk.

....

**Llawhaden, which is near Narberth in
Pembrokeshire, takes its name from
the Welsh for 'Church of St Aidan', after
the sixth-century Irish missionary who
established Lindisfarne Priory, so it is apt
that its castle became a seat for bishops.**

This fortified palace was built by two
Bishops of St Davids, Thomas Bek, who
served from 1280, and Adam de Houghton
from 1361. An earlier earth and timber
ringwork fortress on the site had been
destroyed by Rhys ap Gruffudd in 1193.

A twin-towered gatehouse was later
added and King Henry IV ordered
Llawhaden's reinforcement during
the Glyndŵr uprising.

The castle fell into ruin following the
Dissolution of the Monasteries in the
mid-sixteenth century and the site was
mined for construction material.

....

Pages 136-137: Llawhaden Castle from
above.

Manorbier Castle

Manorbier, Tenby, SA70 7SY.
Constructed 12th century.
www.manorbiercastle.co.uk.

....

Manorbier Castle, just half a mile from the Pembrokeshire shoreline to the south-west of Tenby, was the birthplace of Gerallt Cymro (Gerald of Wales), the twelfth-century clergyman whose written accounts of his journeys through Wales and Ireland made him one of the most important chroniclers of the Middle Ages.

Gerald was born in 1146, the son of William de Barri, who together with his father Odo, one of the original Norman conquerors, was responsible for establishing the first fortress at Manorbier.

Fortified in stone between 1275 and 1375, Manorbier Castle passed unharmed through both major Welsh uprisings of the thirteenth century and only came under attack after a fall-out among the de Barri family itself in 1327.

Ownership of the castle was disputed from the latter part of the fourteenth century and it survived the Owain Glyndŵr uprising unharmed. In 1475 the castle

became the property of the Crown. Garrisoned by Royalists during the English Civil War, Manorbier was surrendered to the Parliamentarians in 1645 after what amounted to only the second assault on the castle in its history. It was slighted and left to ruin.

The castle was acquired in the latter part of the seventeenth century by Sir Erasmus Philipps, a member of parliament and also owner of Picton Castle, near Haverfordwest.

During the eighteenth century, with contraband such as French brandy being landed secretly all along the Pembrokeshire coast, Manorbier Castle's ruins became a hotbed for smuggling and cellars were dug for storage. One smuggler, 'Jolly' Jack Furze, is said to have begun trading here in around 1800 in the everyday guise of a farmer and miner.

Legend has it that after single-handedly piloting his brig, *The Jane*, to a narrow escape from a chasing Revenue ship in gathering darkness one night off Manorbier, Captain Jack turned his back on his law-breaking ways.

As it stands today the castle looks remarkably well-preserved and much of this is down to restoration work carried out in the 1880s at the behest of antiquarian J. R. Cobb, who also undertook grand restorations of the castles in Caldicot and Pembroke. Cobb, who had been granted tenancy of the castle by the Philipps family, refurbished two of the towers into living accommodation.

Pages 138-139: An ariel view over the remains of Manorbier Castle.
Pages 140-141: The gate tower and castle entrance.

Pembroke Castle

Pembroke, Pembrokeshire, SA71 4LA.
Constructed 12th-13th century.
www.pembrokecastle.co.uk.

....

Like Caernarfon before it, Pembroke Castle was the birthplace of an English monarch. Born in 1457 in the tower which now bears his name, Harri Tudur (Henry Tudor) went on to defeat King Richard III at the Battle of Bosworth in 1485 and, as King Henry VII, began a royal dynasty which occupied the throne until 1603.

One of Wales's larger castles, Pembroke rests on a limestone promontory above the River Pembroke, which leads to the Milford Haven waterway in south-west Wales. The Wogan cavern, which lies beneath the castle, has provided evidence of human life on the site dating back at least 10,000 years.

The first wooden fortress at Pembroke was built on an earlier fort raised by Norman baron Roger de Montgomery and his son Arnulf, from 1093. In the twelfth century it held off the army of Rhys ap Gruffudd, the Lord Rhys, as he fought to reclaim the kingdom of Deheubarth and indeed Pembroke Castle was destined never to fall to the Welsh.

The stronghold was fortified in stone during the thirteenth century, first under William Marshal, Earl of Pembroke and a famed knight of the age who served five successive English kings, and then the French nobleman William de Valence. By the time of Owain Glyndŵr's uprising in 1405 it had been sufficiently garrisoned to withstand attack from a French force aligned with Glyndŵr.

After the Tudor era Pembroke Castle's next major brush with history came in 1648, when it was besieged by an army led by Oliver Cromwell. Under the stewardship of John Poyer, a merchant and the mayor of Pembroke, the castle had begun the English Civil War on the side of the Parliamentarians. When Poyer changed his allegiance, however, a decision which would later lead to his execution for treason, Cromwell himself set off with 6,000 men to take the castle from him. After a seven-week siege, Poyer was forced to surrender and the castle was slighted.

In the 1880s antiquarian J. R. Cobb acquired the castle's ruins and, as he did at Caldicot and Manorbier, began to restore them, making significant

improvements to the barbican in the period between 1880-1883. Further reclamation work took place after Sir Ivor Philipps, a British army officer and Member of Parliament, bought the castle in 1928. Following his purchase, an extensive programme of restoration and rebuilding was undertaken, resulting

in the condition in which we find the castle today. Since his death the Phillipps family have jointly managed the site with Pembroke town council.

Pages 142-143: Pembroke Castle is sited on a rocky promontory that extends out into the River Pembroke and surrounded on three sides by water.
Pages 144-145: The keep at Pembroke Castle.

Picton Castle and Gardens

The Rhos, Haverfordwest, Pembrokeshire, SA62 4AS.
Constructed 13th century.
www.pictoncastle.co.uk.

....

Construction of Picton Castle, at Slebech, near Haverfordwest in Pembrokeshire, began in the thirteenth century under Sir John Wogan, Justiciar (or chief governor) of Ireland from 1295-1313, and it has been occupied by his descendants almost ever since.

In the mid-fifteenth century Picton passed to the Dwnn family on the marriage of Katherine Wogan to the poet Owain Dwnn, and then in 1491 it passed to the Philipps family when Joan Dwnn married Sir Thomas Philipps, later sheriff of Pembrokeshire.

Briefly overrun by Royalists in the English Civil War, the castle was remodelled into a mansion in the eighteenth century and remained in the hands of the Philipps family until 1987, when it was gifted to the Picton Castle Trust.

....

Pages 146-147: Reconstruction during the Georgian era transformed Picton Castle into a fine stately home.

Gazetteer

This gazetteer provides an overview of the castles in each of the regions of Wales for easy reference. All entries also include an identifier created by what3words, which encodes geograpic coordinates into three permenantly fixed dictionary words. Find out more at **www.what3words.com**.

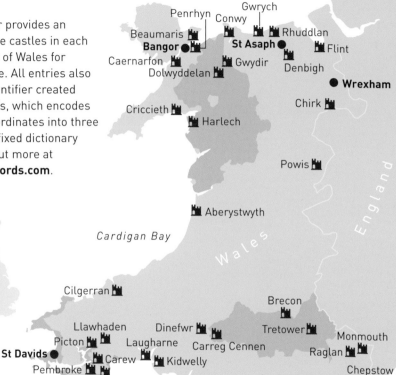

N

Penrhyn
Gwrych
Beaumaris
Conwy
Rhuddlan
Bangor ●
St Asaph ●
Flint
Caernarfon
Gwydir
Dolwyddelan
Denbigh
● **Wrexham**
Criccieth
Chirk
Harlech
Powis
Aberystwyth

Cardigan Bay

W a l e s

England

Cilgerran

Brecon

Llawhaden
Dinefwr
Tretower
Picton
Laugharne
Monmouth
St Davids ●
Carew
Carreg Cennen
Raglan
Pembroke
Kidwelly
Chepstow
Manòrbier
Caerphilly
Caldicot
Swansea ●
Castell Coch
● **Newport**
Ogmore
St Fagans
Cardiff
St Donat's

Bristol Channel

Key
🏰 Castles
● **City**

North Wales

Beaumaris Castle (Page 4)
Castle Street, Beaumaris,
Gwynedd, LL58 8AP.
UNESCO World Heritage Site.
www.cadw.wales.gov.uk.
///even.preparing.blazing

Caernarfon Castle (Page 8)
Castle Ditch, Caernarfon,
Gwynedd, LL55 2AY.
UNESCO World Heritage Site.
www.cadw.wales.gov.uk.
///visual.moon.simple

Conwy Castle (Page 14)
Rose Hill Street, Conwy,
LL32 8AY.
UNESCO World Heritage Site.
www.cadw.wales.gov.uk.
///recruiter.responses.etchings

Criccieth Castle (Page 18)
Castle Street, Criccieth,
Gwynedd, LL52 0DP.
www.cadw.wales.gov.uk.
///moderated.offers.awaited

Denbigh Castle (Page 22)
Castle Hill, Denbigh,
Denbighshire, LL16 3NB.
www.cadw.wales.gov.uk.
///sugars.forgotten.master

Dolwyddelan Castle (Page 26)
Off the A470, Dolwyddelan,
Conwy, LL25 0JD.
www.cadw.wales.gov.uk.
///crinkled.rear.debit

Flint Castle (Page 30)
Castle Road, Flint, Flintshire,
CH6 5PE.
www.cadw.wales.gov.uk.
///embraced.buzzer.glorified

Gwrych Castle (Page 32)
Tan-Y-Gopa Road, Abergele,
Conwy, LL22 8ET.
www.gwrychcastle.co.uk.
///scripted.part.went

Gwydir Castle (Page 36)
Llanrwst, Conwy, LL26 0PN.
www.gwydircastle.co.uk.
///elaborate.ripen.deaf

Penrhyn Castle (Page 40)
Bangor, Gwynedd, LL57 4HN.
www.nationaltrust.org.uk.
///villas.hired.strictest

Rhuddlan Castle (Page 44)
Castle Street, Rhuddlan,
Denbighshire, LL18 5AD.
www.cadw.wales.gov.uk.
///pedicure.sleep.agent

Mid Wales

Aberystwyth Castle (Page 48)
New Promenade, Aberystwyth,
Ceredigion, SY23 2AU.
www.aberystwyth.gov.uk.
///crumbles.doghouse.leads

Brecon Castle (Page 51)
Castle Square, Brecon, Powys,
LD3 9DB.
www.breconcastle.co.uk.
///bring.landmark.unsecured

Chirk Castle (Page 52)
Chirk, Wrexham, LL14 5AF.
www.nationaltrust.org.uk.
///consoled.brand.bench

Harlech Castle (Page 56)
Castle Square, Harlech,
LL46 2YH.
UNESCO World Heritage Site.
www.cadw.wales.gov.uk.
///roost.crumple.album

Powis Castle and Garden
(Page 62)
Welshpool, Powys, SY21 8RF.
www.nationaltrust.org.uk.
///orbited.snow.monkey

Tretower Court and Castle
(Page 68)
Tretower, Crickhowell, Powys,
NP8 1RD.
www.cadw.wales.gov.uk.
///pupils.classed.stiffly

South Wales

Caerphilly Castle (Page 70)
Castle Street, Caerphilly,
CF83 1JD.
www.cadw.wales.gov.uk.
///grace.nasal.nails

Caldicot Castle (Page 76)
Church Road, Caldicot,
Monmouthshire, NP26 4HU.
www.visitwales.com
///ferried.disclose.solve

Cardiff Castle (Page 80)
Castle Street, Cardiff,
CF10 3RB.
www.cardiffcastle.com.
///drum.flat.clues

Castle Coch (Page 88)
Tongwynlais, Cardiff,
CF15 7JS.
www.cadw.wales.gov.uk.
///charmingly.basket.flips

Chepstow Castle (Page 92)
Bridge Street, Chepstow,
Monmouthshire, NP16 5EY.
www.cadw.wales.gov.uk.
///limbs.cutaway.gong

Monmouth Castle (Page 96)
Monmouth, Monmouthsire,
NP25 3BS.
www.cadw.wales.gov.uk.
///duos.wheels.spin

Ogmore Castle (Page 98)
Bridgend, CF32 0QP.
www.cadw.wales.gov.uk.
///loved.scenes.drank

Raglan Castle (Page 100)
Castle Road, Raglan,
Monmouthsire, NP15 2BT.
www.cadw.wales.gov.uk.
///split.loaf.blurs

St Donat's Castle (Page 104)
UWC Atlantic College,
St Donats, Llantwit Major
CF61 1WF.
///snapper.leathers.september

St Fagans Castle (Page 108)
Cardiff, CF5 6XB.
www.museum.wales.
///mixer.small.tree

West Wales

Carew Castle (Page 113)
Castle Lane, Carew, Tenby,
Pembrokeshire, SA70 8SL.
www.pembrokeshirecoast.wales.
///carpeted.fountain.beyond

Carreg Cennen Castle
(Page 116)
Trapp, Llandeilo,
Carmarthenshire, SA19 6UA.
www.cadw.wales.gov.uk.
///reason.winners.routs

Cilgerran Castle (Page 120)
Castle Square, Cilgerran,
Pembrokeshire, SA43 2SF.
www.nationaltrust.org.uk.
///blogs.cycles.masking

Dinefwr Park and Castle
(Page 124)
Llandeilo, Carmarthenshire,
SA19 6RT.
www.nationaltrust.org.uk.
///stuns.retailing.pools

Kidwelly Castle (Page 128)
Castle Road, Kidwelly,
Carmarthenshire, SA17 5BQ.
www.cadw.wales.gov.uk.
///stun.qualified.plant

Laugharne Castle (Page 132)
King Street, Laugharne,
Carmarthen, SA33 4SA.
www.cadw.wales.gov.uk.
///nipped.producers.visitor

Llawhaden Castle (Page 136)
Tal-Y-Bont Hill, Llawhaden,
Narberth, SA67 8HL.
www.cadw.wales.gov.uk.
///poorly.ruled.submerged

Manorbier Castle (Page 138)
Manorbier, Tenby, SA70 7SY.
www.manorbiercastle.co.uk.
///making.roost.crabmeat

Pembroke Castle (Page 142)
Pembroke, Pembrokeshire,
SA71 4LA.
www.pembrokecastle.co.uk.
///workshop.crypt.subject

Picton Castle and Gardens
(Page 146)
The Rhos, Haverfordwest,
Pembrokeshire, SA62 4AS.
www.pictoncastle.co.uk.
///replenish.dabble.newsstand

Useful Information

Cadw

The Welsh Government's historic environment service, working for an accessible and well-protected historic environment for Wales.
www.cadw.gov.wales/visit/places-to-visit/castles-wales

 facebook.com/cadwwales

@cadwcymruwales

@cadwwales

Email: cadw@gov.wales

Tel: 0300 0256000

Castles: Beaumaris (Page 4), Caernarfon (Page 8), Caerphilly (Page 70), Carreg Cennen (Page 116), Castell Coch (Page 88), Cilgerran (Page 120), Conwy (Page 14), Criccieth (Page 18), Denbigh (Page 22), Dolwyddelan (Page 26), Harlech (Page 56), Kidwelly (Page 128), Laugharne (Page 132), Llawhaden (Page 136), Monmouth (Page 96), Ogmore (Page 98), Raglan (Page 100), Rhuddlan (Page 44), Tretower Court and Castle (Page 68).

National Trust

Charity and membership organisation for heritage conservation in England, Wales and Northern Ireland.
www.nationaltrust.org.uk

 facebook.com/NTWales

@ntwales

@NTWales

Email: enquiries@nationaltrust.org.uk

Tel: 0344 8001895

Castles: Cilgerran (Page 120), Chirk (Page 52), Dinefwr (Page 124), Penrhyn (Page 40), Powis (Page 62).

Visit Wales

Welsh Government tourism organisation, promoting Welsh tourism and assisting the tourism industry.
www.visitwales.com

facebook.com/visitwales

@visitwales

@visitwales

Email: enquiries.wales@gov.wales

Brecon Beacons National Park

www.breconbeacons.org

 facebook.com/breconbeaconsnationalpark

@breconbeacons

@BreconBeaconsNP

Email: enquiries@beacons-npa.gov.uk

Tel: 01874 623366

Eryri National Park

www.snowdonia.gov.wales

 facebook.com/parccenedlaetholeryri

@parc_eryri

@eryrinpa

Email: park@snowdonia.gov.wales

Tel: 01766 770274

Pembrokeshire Coast National Park

www.pembrokeshirecoast.wales

 facebook.com/PembrokeshireCoast

@pembscoast

@PembsCoast

Email: info@pembrokeshirecoast.org.uk

Tel: 01646 624800

Carew Castle and Tidal Mill

www.pembrokeshirecoast.wales/carew-castle

facebook.com/carewcastle

@pembscoast

@PembsCoast

Email: enquiries@carewcastle.com

Tel: 01646 651782

Castle of Brecon Hotel

www.breconcastle.com

 facebook.com/Castlehotelbrecon

@thecastlebrecon

@CastleBrecon

Email: castle.brecon@innmail.co.uk

Tel: 01874 624611

Gwrych Castle

www.gwrychcastle.co.uk

 facebook.com/gwyrychcastle

@gwrychcastle

@Gwrych_Castle

Email: info@gwrychcastle.co.uk

Tel: 01745 826023

Gwydir Castle

www.gwydircastle.co.uk

 facebook.com/GwydirCastle

@gwydircastle

@JudyCorbett

Email: info@gwydircastle.co.uk

Tel: 01492 641687

Caldicot Castle

www.monlife.co.uk/heritage/caldicot-castle-country-park

 facebook.com/caldicotcastle

@caldicotcastle

Email: caldicotcastle@monmouthshire.gov.uk

Tel: 01291 420241

Cardiff Castle

www.cardiffcastle.com

 facebook.com/officialcardiffcastle

@cardiff_castle

@cardiff_castle

Email: cardiffcastle@cardiff.gov.uk

Tel: 02920 878100

Manorbier Castle

www.manorbiercastle.co.uk

facebook@Manorbiercastle1

@manorbiercastle

@ManorbierCastle

Email: Manorbiercastleoffice@gmail.com

Tel: 01834 870081

Pembroke Castle Trust

www.pembrokecastle.co.uk

 facebook.com/pembrokecastle.co.uk

 @pembrokecastletrust

@pembscastle

Email: info@pembrokecastle.co.uk

Tel: 01646 681510

Picton Castle Trust

www.pictoncastle.co.uk

facebook.com/PictonCastleGardens

@pictoncastlegardens

@The PictonCastle

Email: info@pictoncastle.co.uk

Tel: 01437 751326

....
St Donat's Castle, UWC Atlantic College

www.uwcatlanticexperience.com

 facebook.com/stdonatscastle

 (dstdonatscastle

Email: info@ucwatlanticexperience.com

Tel: 01446 799000

....
St Fagans Castle, St Fagans National Museum of History

www.museum.wales/stfagans

 facebook.com/stfagansmuseum

 @museumwales

 @StFagans_Museum

Email: post@museumwales.ac.uk

Tel: 0300 1112333

For further books about Wales

visit **graffeg.com/collections/wales-1**

Credits

Castles of Wales.
Published in Great Britain in 2023
by Graffeg Limited.

Designed and produced by Graffeg Limited
copyright © 2023.

Graffeg Limited, 24 Stradey Park Business
Centre, Mwrwg Road, Llangennech, Llanelli,
Carmarthenshire, SA14 8YP, Wales, UK.
Tel 01554 824000. www.graffeg.com.

Rhodri Owen is hereby identified as the author
of this work in accordance with section 77 of
the Copyright, Designs and Patents Act 1988.
A CIP Catalogue record for this book is available
from the British Library.

The publisher gratefully acknowledges the
financial support of this book by the Books
Council of Wales. www.gwales.com.

Printed in China TT14022023

ISBN 9781802584356

1 2 3 4 5 6 7 8 9

Photo credits

© Alamy: Pages 4-5, 8-11, 16-29, 32-43, 47-57,
60-69, 72-102, 104-141, 144-147, back cover:
Harlech Castle and Cardiff Castle. © Cadw:
Pages 70-71. © Drew Buckley: Pages 142-143.
© Istock: Pages 30-31. © Paul E. Williams:
Cover, title, pages 6-7, 14-15, 44-46, 58-59, 103,
back cover: Raglan Castle. © Shutterstock:
Pages 12-13.

The photographs used in this book have come
from a variety of sources. Wherever possible
contributors have been identified although some
images may have been used without credit
or acknowledgement and if this is the case
apologies are offered and full credit will
be given in any future edition.